After our children died, we didn't know if we could even breathe let alone heal from such a tragic event. *Becoming Radiant* is a book we wish was written 19 years earlier. Tom Zuba says it best: "It's making the conscious decision to end the war you have been waging with life. " Everyone in the world experiences death of a loved one. The world needs *Becoming Radiant!*

> Beth Olsen, author and Rick Olsen, author, Shaman, *We Never Left You*

"Brilliance!" Tom has turned grief from unbelievable pain into Love, Light and healing for your soul. *Becoming Radiant* is the truth as to what the Spirit world and your God source wants you and the entire world to know. The Spirit world tells me this everyday with every reading. Thank you Tom.

> Melinda Kushner, Spiritual Medium

Becoming Radiant

A New Way to Do Life

following the "death" of a beloved

Book 2

Tom Zuba

Bish Press
www.TomZuba.com
Rockford, IL USA

Becoming Radiant
A New Way to Do Life
by Tom Zuba

First Printing – July 2018
ISBN 13: 9780692147771

Library of Congress Control Number: 2014956218

Printed in the U.S.A.
0 1 2 3 4 5 6 7 8 9 10 11

ALSO BY TOM ZUBA☐

Permission to Mourn: A New Way to Do Grief

To Ange and Claude Zuba
lovingly
my mom and my dad
the perfect parents for me.
For showing by example
what is most important.
Love. □
Faith.
Family.
Generosity.
Celebrations.
Community.
And yes, yes, yes
a clear understanding of
What Is God?

And to my little brother
Daniel Patrick.
A wise, old soul.
You arrived at the perfect time.
You did everything you came here to do.
Then you dropped your physical body
at the equally-as-perfect time.
And you went home.
To Source. To God.
To Love itself.
Where all things
all things
are possible.
All the while never leaving any of us.
And so it began.

TABLE OF CONTENTS

INTRODUCTION

"The key is to understand that there is nothing we can see or perceive that we are not. If we did not possess a certain quality we could not see it in another. If you are inspired by another's courage, it is a reflection of the courage within you."

~ Debbie Ford, *The Dark Side of the Light Chasers*

Is healing your broken heart - your broken spirit - your broken dream possible? It is. But for me, I don't know that healing is a destination. Not while I'm still in my physical body. My intention, my vision, is that healing now becomes my way of being in the world. I am committed to doing the work of healing every day, knowing I can continue to heal more and more. To me, that's exciting. That's hopeful. That's filled with unlimited possibility. I am not a victim. I am a creator. And as author Byron Katie says, *"Life does not happen to me. It happens for me."* I am loved that much. And so are you. I'm okay with that. Are you?

There are many kinds of dreams. And there are many, many ways our dreams are shattered. Obliterated. Ripped apart. And it's usually painful. Really painful. I've discovered that it's supposed to be. Painful. Unimaginable pain snaps us out of our sleep and into the present moment. The *"point of power"* as author Gary Zukav writes. The place, the only place, where healing can occur.

Indescribable pain gets our attention. It pulls us back into our body. Now. Not the past. Not the future. The present moment. The point of power. Where feelings and emotions exist. Real feelings and emotions. Bearing gifts.

Contrary to what many believe, the feelings and emotions surging through our body are neither good nor bad, right nor wrong, positive or negative, appropriate or inappropriate. They are, however, peaceful or painful; loving or fear-based. They are teachers. Powerful teachers. And when we consciously dive into those feelings and emotions, we find the door we enter to healing. To peace. To love. To radiance.

We've suffered enough. You and I. And I choose peace. As often as I can. You can too.

It's time we do grief a new way, so we can do life a new way. It's time we recognize, realize, remember that every feeling and every emotion is rooted in a belief. A belief we hold on to tightly. Consciously or subconsciously. Pain is not the enemy any more than grief is the enemy. Both are sacred teachers. Pain, a painful feeling, is the door we walk through to create peace. Not avoiding, repressing, denying, pretending or numbing away the pain. The old way to do grief. But walking through that pain. Step by step by step. To encounter truth. To choose peace. Consciously. To shift our perception. To create the miracle. To allow healing. Our broken heart. Our broken spirit. Our broken dream.

To become radiant.

If you are drowning in deep, deep, deep pain, please read my book *Permission to Mourn: A New Way to Do Grief* first. Read it again. And again. Roll around in it. Marinate in it. Discuss it. Try it on for size. Adjust, nip, tuck, play with its content, it's teachings until it fits you perfectly. Inhale it until you, too, know that healing is possible. Until you see tangible signs of healing - in yourself. Until you understand what a miracle is. Really. And you know how to create one. Many. On the inside. Of you.

When you have a clear understanding of What Your God Is. And when you know, at a deep, deep level, that The Relationship Continues and that Words Have Power and that the way you consciously choose to Tell Your Story creates peace or pain, then you are ready for this book. Then you are ready. Really ready.

It may take a day. A week. A month. A year. A handful of years. Decades to be ready. It's not a race. We are each responsible for our own healing. And author Caroline Myss teaches that, *"We each determine the speed at which we heal."*

You will know when you are ready for *Becoming Radiant.* Trust your gut. Your intuition. Your heart. Trust your body. Your God-given-barometer recognizes truth by the way it feels. Truth feels expansive. Trust that.

I wrote this book for you. To remind you that you did not come to the planet to suffer. Neither did I. We came to be radiant. Not in spite of the fact that our dreams have been shattered, but because of the fact that our dreams have been shattered. Not in spite of the fact that someone we love dearly has "died." But because of the fact that someone we love dearly has "died."

We came here to be radiant.

Take my hand. Let's begin together. We have suffered enough.

There is a new way to do life.

With much, much love,
Tom

1. *THE INVITATION*

To become
who you have never been
you must do
what you have never done.

This is the challenge.
The intention.
The prayer.
The vision.
This is the work.
The action.
The opportunity.
The hope.
The promise.
This is the invitation.

The invitation.

This is what will give
the seemingly incomprehensible
meaning
and purpose.

To go against everything
and almost everyone.

To trust.
Your self.
To trust your very self.

To believe.
To choose to believe
that which we call
the death of our beloved
is not the end.
It is not.
Rather to believe
to choose to believe
that the death
the death of your beloved
is actually the beginning.
Of you.
Of you *really* living life
a new way
here on earth.
Now.

And to choose to believe
that death is the continuation
in a most dynamic way
of the relationship that exists
now and forever
between you
and the ones you love
so dearly.

To choose to believe that
the relationship continues.
It does.

And to believe -
to choose to believe -
that which we call death

is simply the next
glorious
love-infused
perfect chapter
for your beloved.
And for you.

To go against everything
and almost everyone.
To make your own way.

To do
what you have never done.
in order to become
who you have never been.

That is the invitation.

2. THE CHOICE

There is no going back
ever
to the person you were
before the person you love
dearly
died.

Many
many
many
parts of that person
the person you were
before
died
too.
There is no going back.

You now have three choices.

1. You may choose to remain stagnant.
Stuck between.
Eventually you will rot from the inside out.
You will have much company in this place.
This stagnant place.
And yes
this is a choice
which you are free to make.

2. You may choose to fall deeper

and deeper
and deeper
still
into the dark pit
where
anger
sadness
regret
hopelessness
despair
guilt
vengefulness
and hatred
will eat you alive.
Eventually.
This does not just happen.
This
too
is a choice.
A choice
you make over
and over
and over again.
And yes
you will have plenty of company here
too.

3. Or you can choose to live.
Life.
Your life.
Your new life.
A combination of who you were
before

and who you consciously choose to become
now.
Day
by day
by day.
You can choose to live
life
your life
not in spite of the fact
that someone you love
dearly
has died
but
because of the fact
that someone you love
dearly
has died.

Yes
this too
is a choice.
An often difficult choice.
At first.
A choice that requires a tremendous amount of work.
And courage.
And tenacity.
And determination.
And a willingness to open to grace.

I believe it is grace
that brought you to this book
to this page
to reading these words.

I believe that it is grace
that will light your way.
If
and when
you say yes.

So
say yes.
Over
and over
and over again.

At times
you will discover
that saying no
is actually your way of saying yes
to you.

There is a small
growing circle of humans
making this choice.

They are choosing to say yes
to life.
Their life.
Following the death of their beloved.
They are saying yes
because when they say no
they realize
that they are creating
pain
on top of pain
on top of pain.

And they have decided
that they have experienced
enough pain.

They have experienced enough pain.

You will recognize each other by
your gentleness with life.
By your willingness to try to forgive
everyone
for everything
every time.
You will recognize each other
by your compassion
and your love.

But most of all
you will recognize each other
by the way you feel
feel
feel
feel
when you are in each other's presence.

There will be a radiant light
shining from your eyes
where there was once
darkness
and despair
and hopelessness.

You will feel more alive
than you have ever felt before

when you are in each other's company.

And you will fall to your knees
in gratitude
as you remember a time
when you did not believe
that feeling so alive
would ever be possible again.

Say yes.
Choose to live.
Choose to live your life.
Your life.
Your new life.

Say yes
to becoming radiant.

It's exactly why you came to the planet.

3. IS HEALING POSSIBLE?

Is healing possible?
And if it is
what does it look like?
Feel like?
Taste like?
Smell like?
Sound like?

Yes.
I believe healing is possible.
But I'm not sure it's a destination
we'll arrive at one day.
I'm not certain we'll wake up one day
and say
Done with that.
I'm all healed now.

Rather
for me
and for you
healing becomes
our way of being in the world.
Our intention
our hope
our prayer
is that we heal
more
and more
with each passing day.

The truth is
we each decide if we will heal.
It's a decision we make
over
and over
and over again.
And remarkably
we each determine the speed at which we heal.
We each determine the speed.

You think you are broken.
Maybe you are
and maybe you aren't.
Not really.

You are
however
most certainly broken open.
Broken open
because someone you love
dearly
died.
And this death
this one
was not part of the plan
you had created
for the rest of your life.

Your plan
your dream
your hope
your vision

your future
your life
has been broken.

Open.
Wide open.

Is it possible to make peace with life
your life
again
or for the first time
following the death of someone you love
so dearly?

It is.

It is possible.

Will you go back to the life you had?
To being the person you were?
To believing all the things you did
before
the person you love
so dearly
died?

No.
That is not possible.

It will require a herculean effort
on your part
to heal.
Herculean.

It is not easy.
And that is why many
(most)
do not do it.
They don't heal.
It's just too hard.
For them.

But you are here.
Reading these words.
Because a part of you -
the soul part of you -
is looking for truth.

You will recognize truth when you encounter it.

In order to heal
you must return to love.
You must return to the very
very
very core
the center
of the relationship you have
still and forever
with the person you love
so dearly
who died.

And the path you must take to that center
to that core
to that love
is through
not around

the sadness
anger
anguish
despair
guilt
rage
regret
loneliness
confusion
terror
and every other feeling and emotion
that the death of your beloved triggers.

You must go through.
Not around.

You must learn to love your self.
You must learn to love yourself
so very much
that you will no longer create pain
by holding on to
all that has been causing you pain
these days
weeks
months
years
decades.
You must forgive
and then release
all of it.
For you.

It begins with setting the intention.

I wish I believed I could heal.

I believe I could heal.

I believe I will heal.

I can heal.

I am healing.

This is what healing looks like.
And feels like.
And tastes like.
And smells like.
And this is what healing sounds like.

It's making the conscious decision to end the war
you have been waging with life.
Your life.
It's being willing and able to practice living life as it is
and not as you wish it would be
or think it should be.
It's surrendering.
Not giving up
but surrendering to what is.

It's beginning to forgive everyone
for absolutely everything.
For what they said
and for what they didn't say.
For what they did
and for what they didn't do.

Healing feels like moving out of deep
deep
deep sadness
into a space of gratitude.
Being grateful that your beloved came at all.
That she touched your life.
And that you touched hers.
Deeply
and profoundly.
Being grateful that they love you
and that you love them.
Still.
Healing is being able to look at photos
and videos
and smiling
and laughing
and remembering
and feeling
with deep gratitude.

It's noticing the colors of life
again.

It's enjoying a cup of coffee.

Healing is becoming comfortable in your own skin.
Again
or for the first time.

And feeling passionate about something.
About someone.
About yourself.

You know you are healing when you can say yes.
Much more often than you say no.
To life.
To love.
To yourself.

Healing is feeling hopeful.
And looking forward.

It's figuring out why you came to the planet.

Healing gives meaning
and purpose
to all you've lived through.

And healing is being able to sit
just sit
with the next person who hears the devastating
life-changing
unimaginable news
that their beloved
finished all the work
he came here to do.
Dropped his physical body
And returned home.

Healing is not easy.
It is hard
hard
hard
hard work.
It requires a herculean effort
over

and over
and over again.

And part of you is ready
or you would not be reading these words.

To heal
you must give yourself
permission to mourn.

Healing is not easy.
But it is possible.
And oh
is it worth the effort.

4. *SET THE INTENTION TO HEAL*

I invite you to commit
today
to healing your broken heart
your broken dreams
your broken life.
I invite you to set the intention to heal.

I'm not certain that healing is a destination.
Rather
now
for you and for me
healing can become our way of being in the world.
I'm okay with that.
Are you?

The hope
the prayer
the intention
is that we heal a little bit more each day.
Remembering that time -
alone -
does not
does not
does not heal all things.
What matters
is what we do with that time.
What we do
consciously
and subconsciously

is what determines
whether or not we will heal.

And
we each determine the speed at which we heal.

I invite you to re-engage with life
today.
Your life
Exactly as it is.
Perfect in its seeming imperfections.
Decide to re-engage in even the smallest way.

I invite you to re-engage with life.
Even if just for a few moments.

Can you do that?
Will you do that?

I invite you to find one thing
one thing
that stops you in your tracks
jolts you into the present moment
the only point of power
and makes you feel
even the tiniest bit
better
than you have been feeling.

I invite you to step out of your story.
Your story of
someone I love
dearly

died
and notice
life.
Notice life.

Just for a few moments
notice the life that's all around you today.
If noticing is even possible.

I want you to plant seeds today.
Of hope.
Plant seeds of hope.
Of possibility.
Of new life.
In you.

What makes you smile?
Or what made you smile
before
the person you love
dearly
died?

I love coffee.
First thing in the morning.
And when I stop myself
and get present
I can close my eyes
and savor the aroma of coffee.
With real whipping cream.
And that helps my heart smile.
Still.
When I'm fully present.

What makes you smile?
What makes your heart skip a beat?
Find it.
Today.

Is it a certain song?
A musical artist?
A type of music?
Marinate in that today.
Give yourself permission to smile.

Is it a favorite book?
A book of poems?
The Bible?
A photograph?
A painting?
A photo album?
A home video?
A coffee table art book?
Immerse yourself in that.
Give yourself permission to smile today.

Is it sitting in his favorite chair.
Wrapping yourself in her robe.
Getting really
really still
and actually feeling his arms around you?
Do that.
Today.
Is it the scent of a certain flower?
A perfume?
An aftershave?
A candle?

Marinate in that scent.
Breathe it in.
Smile.
If even for just a moment.

The point of power
is the present moment.
This present moment.
Not the past.
Not the future.
The present moment.
Where healing occurs.

What will you do today?
One thing.
That stops you in your tracks
jolts you into the present moment
and makes you feel
even the tiniest bit
better
more peaceful
than you have been feeling.

What will you do today
to heal?

5. YOU CAN BECOME MORE. NOT LESS.

Grief is not the enemy.
Grief is the teacher.

But its lessons are not learned in the head.
With the mind.
Its lessons are heart lessons.
Love-centered.
Filtered through grace.
Its gifts.
Yes
gifts
are received through the heart.

Over
and over
and over
again
your mind will say
But this is not fair.
I don't deserve this.
Why me?
I will never get over this.
The pain will always be here.

Don't get trapped
by the vicious
repetitive

voices
in your mind.

Healing grief is not a head thing.

Healing grief is a heart thing.

And when the heart speaks to you
in silence
it says
I know darkness
deep
all-encompassing
seemingly endless
often frightening
darkness
so I will be light
for the next person.

And the heart says
I know loneliness
too.
Even in
(especially in)
a room full of people
so I will be a friend
for the next person.

And the heart says
I know terror.
Indescribable
inexplicable
terror

so I will be comfort
for the next person.

And the heart says
I know despair
too.
Paralyzing
can't-get-out-of-bed
life is too dark
despair
so I will be hope
for the next person.

As you do the grace-filled work of healing
you begin to realize
first
in your heart
that you are more
of who you were
not less.

You can become more.
Not less. □
By the choices you make.

We think that grief is the enemy
to be avoided at all costs.
It is not.
Grief is not the enemy.
Grief is the great life-giving teacher.

Grief is the bearer
of powerful

transformative
love-centered gifts.
Gifts.

Not in spite of the fact that someone you love died.
But because of the fact that someone you love died.

Grief is the teacher.
The life-giving
heart-expanding
teacher.
Grief is the teacher
when you choose to say yes
to life
to love
to your beloved,
to your very self.

Grief is not the enemy.

Say yes.

6. *MOURNING*

Everyone grieves differently.

No one should tell me how to grieve.

There isn't a right way to grieve and a wrong way to grieve.

Every day
you can read these statements
and different versions of these statements
all over the internet.
They are almost declarations of
Don't you dare mess with my grief.
I get to do it my way.

I am quite certain
that early in this 25+ year grief journey of mine
I said the exact same things.

And while I agree
100%
that each person gets to do grief
however he or she wants
I think we do ourselves
and each other
a disservice
when we don't acknowledge
that there are healthy ways to do grief
and there are unhealthy ways to do grief.

Peaceful ways and painful ways.

And in each of the statements above
grieve
a verb
is referring to one's response to grief.
How they do grief.

Everything changed for me
shortly after my son Rory died in 2005
when I decided to define grief as
the internal
automatic
response to the end of a dream.
In defining grief this way
as the internal automatic response to a dream ending
it became clear that everyone -
yes everyone -
is living with grief
because everyone is experiencing different types
and intensities of
dreams ending every day.
Grief itself isn't right or wrong.
Grief just is.
Grief is what happens inside of us.
And the truth is
we all have much more in common
in our grief experiences
than we've been led to believe.

Grief expresses itself
in hundreds
and hundreds

of often surprising and confusing ways. □
Surprising and confusing
because we never talk about it.
Until now.

Some of the ways grief expresses itself include
feeling sad
angry
jealous
panic-stricken
exhausted
desperate
lonely
abandoned
confused
frightened
dizzy
regretful
lost
forgotten
neglected
wounded
forgetful
disoriented.
Grief looks like
overeating
not eating at all
sleeping all day
not being able to sleep

Grief feels numb
like it's a dream
heart palpitations

like you're having a heart attack
etc.
etc.
etc.

Grief makes you wonder
Am I going crazy?

And remarkably
you may experience all of these feelings and emotions
at the same time
or in a matter of moments
or over
and over
and over again.

Grief
especially at first
when it is new
and fresh
often feels like a tsunami
wreaking havoc inside of you
and like a volcano erupting
over
and over
again.
Grief is like a twister
a tornado
a Category 5 hurricane
tossing
and turning
and destroying everything in its path.

We are all living with grief.
And we all have much more in common
in that grief
than we realize.
Realizing that our grief can bring us together
instead of pushing us apart
can help us feel less alone.
That realization
that we have much more in common
than
at first
we might have thought
in itself
is healing.

I believe there is a healthy response to grief.
A healthy way to do grief.
And I believe there is an unhealthy response to grief.
An unhealthy way to do grief.

There is a response that will help us heal
and a response that will keep us stuck.
Drowning in a seemingly bottomless
hopeless
pit of despair.
And each person is free
to choose to respond to grief
whichever way he or she likes.

I think it's helpful
for those who are choosing
to respond to grief
in an unhealthy

un-healing way
to be aware of the options.

If you want to heal
you must mourn.

You must push the grief up and out.
You must actively engage with your grief.
As painful as it is
and it is painful.

You must feel it.
You must express it.
You must dance with it
wrestle with it
and immerse yourself in it.
And then you must release it
and allow it to release you.

You must do grief a new way.
You must mourn.

In order to heal
you must mourn.

How does one mourn?
How do we push the grief up and out?

There are many
many
many ways.

First

set the intention to heal.
Declare it.
Let healing be your goal
your prayer
your motivator.
Let healing
be your new reason
to get out of bed each morning.

Second
create a vision.
What does healing
your healing
look
sound
feel
taste
and smell
like for you?

Third
you must take action.

You must do grief.
You must engage.
Feel.
Express.
Allow.
Honor.

How?

Talk about grief.

Over and over and over.

Paint it.
Draw it.
Form it in clay.
Art is a powerful
healing way to express
and process
that which you might not be able to express
through words.

Dance it.
Move it.
Release grief by shaking your body.

Beat it out on a drum.

Write it out.
In a journal.
In a poem.
In your blog.
In a letter to yourself.
In a letter to your beloved
the one who has died.
☐
In a letter from your beloved
to you.
Yes
a letter to you
from the one you love
who died.

Sing it out.

Compose your own song.

Play it out.
On an instrument.
Guitar.
Flute.
Violin.
Piano.

Exercise it out.
CrossFit.
Zumba.
At your gym.
On a stationary bike.
On a StairMaster.
In a pool.

Run it out
bike it out
walk it out.

Yoga it out.

Meditate it out.

Scream
shout
wail it out.

The healthy
healing
response to grief
if you want to heal

is to mourn.

Give yourself permission to mourn.

7. STEPPING INTO THE FIRE

You may moan
and groan
and kick
and scream
and shout
and foam at the mouth for as long as you like.

Forever actually.
if you so choose.
As many do.

You may tell us all
over
and over
and over again
how unfair life is.
How you hate being
in a club no one wants to be in.

You may tell us as often as you like
that your loved one was robbed of living a full life.
That you've been robbed.
That your kids have been robbed.
Hell
you can tell us that the whole world has been robbed
because your beloved died
way
way
way too soon.

You can tell us that death sucks.
You can wear it on a t-shirt
and print it on a mug
and have it stenciled as a border
on your dining room walls if you like.

You can tell us that you have a hole in your heart
your being
your life
that will never be full again.
Never.

You can tell us that no one understands you.
Or you can tell us that the only people who understand you
are those who experienced the same kind of death.
Of a child.
A spouse.
A drug overdose.
A suicide.
Or whatever kind of death you are living with.

You can tell us that the death you experienced is the worst.
The most painful.
The most cruel.

You can tell us that you did
indeed
lose your beloved.

It's your choice.
You can have all of that.
For as long as you like.

Or you can let the flames of grief
mold
and shape
and create a new version of you.
The you
you were born to become.
The highest version of you.

This requires courage.
Strength.
Trust when there is no reason on earth
you would trust anyone
or anything
again.

This requires stepping right into the flames
of grief.

This asks you to feel the pain.
To allow it.
To honor it.
To make room for it.
To be with it.
This is not easy.

This is about believing
somehow
someway
that you have not been abandoned,
That you are not alone.
Not really.

This asks you to trust

that in the center
the very center of the flames
is your understanding of God.
And your beloved.
The one you love who has died.
Both forces
together
waiting for you with outstretched arms.

This is how you heal.

By stepping into the fire.

Your job is to find
your version of God
and your beloved
in the center of the fire.

There is a new way to do life.
Your life.
And a part of you is ready.
or you wouldn't be reading these words.

Feed that part.

8. IT'S NOT PERSONAL

It is essential that you realize
and remember
which is why I am telling you
that the world we have collectively created
the world we live in
is one where very shortly after the one you love dies
you will feel like you have been abandoned
by many
many
many people.

People you love.
People you thought loved you.

People you trusted
and counted on.

People you shared your life with.

People who knew
and loved
your beloved.

People who you are certain
you would not abandon
if the tables were turned
and they were the ones
whose beloved had died.

It is also essential that you realize
and remember
that this is not personal.

It has nothing to do with you.
This abandonment thing.

It's what we do.
Certainly we do it in the United States
but I am learning that people do this all over the globe.

When people need us the most
we abandon them.

This abandonment thing is not personal.
This has nothing to do with you
and everything to do with the person -
the people -
who are abandoning you.

Simply put
it is about them
not you.
Do you get that?
Let that sink in.

You did nothing wrong.
You said nothing wrong.
Someone you love
dearly
died.

You have to make a decision.

How important is this person
or these people
to you?
How important is it to you
to have them in your life?
The rest of your life?
The life you are creating
after the person you love
died?

Do you want them in
or are you okay if they are out?

Because if you want them in
you will have to speak up.

You will have to become the teacher.
You will have to very
very
very
clearly explain
from a place of love
exactly what it is you need.

Explain what you need.
Explain what you want.
Explain what would be helpful
to you.
Explain what they can do
and say
to help make life easier.

In order to change the way we do grief

and care for those who are doing grief
worldwide
we must speak up.

We must speak up
when
and if
we are
ready and able.

We must begin walking down a new path.
Together.
And you must lead.

How else will the others know?

You must become the teacher.

You must commit
to transforming the way we do grief
worldwide.

This grief stuff
is very
very
very
hard work.

If you are willing to do the work
the work of healing
instead of doing grief the old way
denying
repressing

pretending
and doing all kinds of things to stay numb
you will discover
that healing is possible.

It may
however
take longer
for you to heal
than many of your family members expect.
And way
way
way longer
than many of your friends expect
or even allow.

This grief stuff is hard work.

In order to heal
you need a safe
sacred
space.

A space where you get to feel
every feeling and every emotion that arises.
And if you're not repressing
denying
pretending
or going numb
the feelings
and the emotions arising
can feel like a volcano erupting.
Like a tsunami destroying everything in it's path.

Like a Category 5 hurricane.
All the time.
Day and night.

In order to heal
you must feel loved and lovable.☐

And when those you thought loved you
abandon you
running as far away
as quickly as they can
you don't feel loved.
Or lovable.

Hard as it is
please remember
that the problem is not you.
It is not personal.
It is them.
Not you.
They can't handle real life.
Because you
my friend
are in the midst of living a real life.

This grief stuff
is about as real as it gets.

In order to heal
you must be seen
heard
and honored
exactly as you are.

Right now.
In this moment.

You don't need to be fixed.
Or given unsolicited advice.

You need to be accompanied.
You need someone to sit on the bench next to you.

This grief stuff.
Is hard.

It's really
really
really
really
really hard work.

So for today
don't give up.
Do not give up.
Do not give up.

You are the only one who knows what you really need to heal.
You are the only one.

What is it?
What do you need today to heal?
Can you give that to yourself?
Will you?

Sometimes saying yes
to you

is actually saying no to someone else.
And that is okay.

It is okay to say no
to those who have abandoned you.
It is okay to say no
to those who ran away.

They did the best they could.
But for you
it wasn't good enough.
It wasn't what you needed.
So you can say no.
With love.
For now.

9. COMPLICATED GRIEF

What if I told you
that the appropriate
natural
healthy
and even healing response
when someone you love dearly dies
is to kick
scream
roll around on the floor
and foam at the mouth?
Until you no longer have a need to do that.

Well
it is.

But instead of the kicking
and screaming
the rolling and foaming
your doctor may now encourage you
to take a pill to
take the edge off of it.

No need to feel the pain
he or she may say
when there's a little pill for that.

Grief is not depression.
Nor is grief one of the many conditions
appropriately treated by prescribed

and properly monitored
medication.

Grief is grief.
The internal
automatic response to the end of a dream.

And instead of honoring
all the ways that grief expresses itself
many of us have bought into the mythical
iconic images of a graceful
dignified
and somehow through her black veil
still beautiful Jackie Kennedy
navigating her husband's funeral and burial.
Images that travelled around the world
and continue to hold power over us.

By doing so
we've unknowingly
and subconsciously
set ourselves up to create pain
on top of pain.

It's become the American way to do grief.
Pretending.
Denying.
Repressing.
Numbing.
Staying strong.
And sucking it all up.

I call it the old way of doing grief.

Trust me.
It doesn't work.
I tried it.
My 18-month-old daughter Erin died suddenly in 1990.
My 43-year-old wife Trici died equally as suddenly in 1999
and my 13-year-old son Rory died of brain cancer in 2005.

In our attempt to get back to
the way things were
as quickly as possible
we've shortened our sacred rituals
surrounding death.
We now need to wrap it up
and tie it with a bow
in three days or less.
Most of us have to be back at work.

A two or three-day visitation and funeral
where immediate family
was supported by extended family
friends
and neighbors
has conveniently morphed into a quick and easy
one-stop
no muss
no fuss
sign the book so they know you were there
walk past the dead body
or better yet
the ashes in a pretty urn
shake a hand with a bumbled
my deepest condolences
and you're back home in 15 minutes

or so
if you timed it right.

We will do anything
and everything possible
to make sure we never have to feel a feeling
or express an emotion.

And now we've decided
that grief is the enemy.
A sickness.
A disease.
We need to label it
and dissect it
and give it a time period
365 days
before it becomes
complicated.

We're being told that women have a harder time
and are more susceptible to
catching
complicated grief.

Same scenario
if the death of your beloved was sudden
or by suicide
or your beloved was a child
or God forbid
you've had multiple *losses*.

Grief is the automatic
internal response

to the end of a dream.

If you are human
and you attach to people
places
or things
a beloved
your job
your house
your car
your health
your youth, etc.
That dream will end.

You will grieve.
Everyone grieves.
All the time.

And grief expresses itself in
countless number of confusing and surprising ways.

Sadness
and anger
and guilt
and numbness
and confusion.

Grief expresses itself through overeating
or losing your appetite
through heart palpitations
and dizziness.
Through loss of memory
and a strong desire to stay in bed

or to work all the time
or just sit in a chair and stare.
This is all grief.

Most of us don't know much about it.
How would we?
We pretend it doesn't exist.
We never talk about it
until it is our turn to navigate the journey.

Although
the very nature of grief is wild
and unpredictable
and nonlinear
and yes
complicated.
Grief is not the enemy.

Grief is not to be avoided at all costs.
Grief can be the great teacher
when we let it.

We heal when we mourn.
When we identify what is occurring on the inside
and push it up and out.
This is the new way to do grief.

We mourn when we externalize the internal.
The problem
however
is that most of us are given three to five days
to mourn
and then it's back to work

and back to *normal.*

It's the message we are given
over
and over
and over again
from our boss
our family members
our friends
and our colleagues.
They don't know any better
and won't until it is their turn.
They are innocent and ignorant.

When someone we dearly love dies
a part of us dies too.
The part dies that was wrapped up
in the plans
and wishes
and dreams we had
for our life with our beloved
be that a child
a spouse or partner
a parent
sibling
or a dear family member
or friend.

Life will never go back to the way it was.

The challenge
the opportunity
is to create a new life.

A life that is richer
because we are capable of loving
deeply.
A life that is more compassionate
and kinder
and more gentle.
A life filled with gratitude for what is.

Healing occurs when we mourn in a safe
sacred space
where we get to feel every feeling
and every emotion that arises.
A space where we feel loved
and lovable.

A space where we are seen
heard
and honored exactly as we are.
Today.
In this moment.

Sadly
we no longer create this space for ourself
and we certainly don't create this space
for each other.
Therefore
most of us no longer mourn.

And that's why our grief journey
may get complicated.
It's not the grief that's complicated.
Grief is natural and normal.

It's the lack of understanding
love
compassion
kindness
gentleness
and the willingness
to accompany another person on their journey
that complicates the journey.

We can do better.
There is a new way
and it is rooted in deep
deep
deep love.

Of self.
And of other.

There is a new way to do grief
which creates a new way to do life.

10. ASK □

I still believe that most people
most of us
are basically good.
Do you believe that?

I believe that if one of our friends
someone we really cared about
asked us to help them
if we could
we would.
Offer our help.
Our assistance.
Do you believe that too?

Someone you love
dearly
has died.
And right now
life may be way
way
way too difficult
for you to navigate all by yourself.

It is okay to ask for help.
It is.
You do not have to do this all by yourself.

Trust me
I know you already feel fragile

and vulnerable
and not your *old self.*
You may be
frightened by life.
Your life.
You may feel a paralyzing terror.

All the more reason to ask for help.

I know you may feel abandoned.
Forgotten.
Pushed aside.
Left behind
left out
and not included anymore.
I know you may feel invisible.
As if nobody cares.

But I have to believe
still
that there are people in your life
who want to help
you.
They just don't have a clue
how
to help you.
They don't know what to do.

So you have to ask.
For help with the taxes.
Or with spring yard work.
Or to get new tires on the car.
Or with babysitting for an evening or a weekend afternoon.

You have to ask for what you need.
Someone to walk with.
Or have coffee with.
Or see a movie with.
Or to go to lunch with.

You have to ask
about that noise in the house
the smoke from the car
or that leaky faucet.

You don't have to do it all by yourself.

I have to believe
that if the roles were reversed
and they asked you for help
you'd say yes.

Ask.
Give someone the opportunity to say yes.
To you.

11. WHERE DO YOU LIVE?

The most important decision
we make
is whether we believe
in a friendly
or hostile universe. ~ Albert Einstein

While in his physical body
my son Rory
loved all things Albert Einstein.

When Rory was six-years-old
he turned to his mother and me
and said
Whoever dies first.
When you get to heaven and meet Einstein.
Tell him to come visit me in my dreams.
I have some questions for him.

When Rory was seven-years-old his mother died.
I have no doubt she fulfilled his request.

When someone we love
dearly
dies
we are thrust into the deepest
darkest
seemingly bottomless
pit
of despair

confusion
pain
and hopelessness.
This is grief.

If
and when possible
it is important
and helpful
to remain as still as we can.
In that darkness.
So we can get our bearings.
Again.
Or for the first time.

At some point
if we're paying attention
we realize that we've been cracked open.
That is precisely
what the death of a beloved
does to us.
It is supposed to.
We are supposed to be cracked open.

And when
and if
we are able to stop resisting what Is -
for even a moment or two -
questions arise.
At first we might not see these questions.
Or hear them.
Or feel them.

That does not matter.
The questions will continue to arise.
They have a life of their own.
In fact
these questions are life itself
dancing with us.

And one of the questions
the starting point I think
is
Is there a God?

Is there a God?
Or a Higher Power
or The Force
or the All of the All
or the Great Unknown
or Nature itself
or the Universe
or whatever you decide to call him/her/it/they.

I am convinced that God does not care what name we use.

I have decided
and it's a decision I had to make over
and over
and over again.
Especially at first.
And sometimes even now.
Still.
That God is Love.
Simple.
Complex.

God is Love.

Not a limited
small
human kind of love
but rather
a love that I simply can't comprehend.
An unconditionally unconditional love.
A radiant
light-filled
limitless
no boundary
indescribable
you-have-to-experience-it-to-know-it
kind of love.

That's what I have decided to believe my "God" is.

So when I revisit Einstein's quote:
"The most important decision we make ☐
is whether we believe in a friendly or hostile universe."
I believe I live in a friendly universe.
Even on
especially on
the days it doesn't feel so friendly.
In order to heal
we must each set the intention to heal.
I can heal.
I will heal.
I am healing.

And then we have to decide where we live.
In a friendly or a hostile universe?

As I wrote in Chapter 14 of
Permission to Mourn
Words.
Have.
Power.
It's the language you use
to describe the death of your loved one
that tells the story.

The story of whether or not you will heal.

And your language is deeply rooted in your beliefs.

So
what is it for you?
Where do you live?
In a friendly
or a hostile universe?
Friendly
or hostile?

Your answer
is rooted
deeply
in your understanding
of
your version of God.

12. SURRENDER TO THE MYSTERY

When someone you love
dearly
dies
the battle of all battles begins.
You wage war with life.
Your life.

I did.

Our natural instinct
seems to be to resist what IS.
To resist
to push back
to fight
this new life.
Your new life.

Surrendering to the new truth
that someone you love
dearly
has died
may feel like you are allowing it to be real.
To be true.
And that is the last thing you want to happen.
For any of this to be real.
We want to keep reality at bay
for as long as we can.
So we use as much energy as we can

to wage war.

Most of us keep doing this
until the pain we are experiencing
is so overwhelming
we can't fight another second.
We don't have it in us.

And
bit
by bit
by bit
we surrender.
To what IS.

We lay
outstretched on the floor
literally
or figuratively
and say
I surrender.
I surrender.
I surrender.

Not to give up.
But to stop fighting.
Reality.

The war we have been waging ends.

And when the embers stop burning.
And the smoke clears.
And the heat cools.

We look around
slowly
and ask ourself
Now what?
Now what?
Now what?

A new way to do life emerges.
Out of the embers.

13. THIS IS NOT THE END

If you are reading these words
you are part of the tribe
that has come to the planet
at this time in history
to change the way we do grief.

You are learning
that the death of your loved one
is not the end.
It is the beginning.
The beginning
of a new way of being
for you.

And that new way of being
includes a new relationship
with the person you love
who finished all the work
he came here to do
left their physical body
and returned home.

The relationship continues.

It does not matter if he was here for one minute
one day
six years
32 years
or 101 years.

It does not matter if her precious body
was never actually born alive.

The relationship continues.

The essence of who I am
and the essence of who you are
is eternal.
We are each spiritual beings having a physical experience.
When we are done here on earth
we go home.
To Source.
To God.
To Love.
When we are done.
We all go home.

You are not done.
And neither am I.
How do we know that?
We are each still here.

So the invitation
following the transition of your beloved
is to discover
why you are still here.

Why are you here?
Why are you still here in your physical body?

Grief is your teacher.
Grief is not your enemy.
You are learning consciously

or subconsciously.
You are awake
or still asleep.
And you are choosing to be
bitter
angry
hopeless
and
closed off
or you are choosing to be
grateful
gentle
hope-filled
and
open-hearted.

What are you learning?
Who are you becoming?
The choice is yours.
Always.
The choice is yours.

14. *YOU ARE NOT ALONE*

Some of the *experts*
and some of the authors
the poets and songwriters
the television shows
and some of the movies.

Even some of the others who are on this same path
have led us to believe that we are all alone.

We have been told
over
and over
and over again
that we are on our own.
That we must find our own way.
That our path
is
unique
different
separate.

And while some of that is true.
Much of it is not.

What they failed to tell us
is that when we talk about our journey□
our journey through grief
honestly
openly

authentically
completely
and with great vulnerability,
we realize
(often for the first time)
that we are not alone.
That
we are not
going
crazy.

That we have much more in common
on this trek through the wilderness
of grief
than we first realized -
than we have been told.

And this new awareness
itself
is healing.

This new awareness
gives
us
hope.

We are not alone.
We have more in common than we know.
Much more.
Those of us
who are learning to live
with the death of someone we love.

Most of us yearn to know if our beloved still exists.
In some shape
form
place.
Most of us yearn to know if our beloved is safe
and whole
and healthy
and happy.
Most of us yearn to know if they can communicate with us.
And we with them.
Most of us feel
lost
frightened
hopeless
angry
confused.
Most of us feel so much sadness
that the person we love has died
that we are afraid to allow ourselves
to feel
that sadness
for fear
we will not
recover.
We fear that the sadness
will swallow
us up.
Forever.
Most of us feel abandoned
by family.
By friends.

So most of us shut down

Because there is no safe place to talk
honestly
openly
authentically
completely
and with great vulnerability.

There is no place where we can be
exactly
who we are.
Today.
Right now.

So we continue to believe the lie.
We continue to believe that we are all alone.
In the wilderness.

We are not.
Alone.

We have much more in common
than we have been led to believe.
And that awareness
itself
is healing.

15. *CRYING*

Crying.

The natural
normal
cleansing
healthy
healing
release
and
physical response
when someone we love
dearly
dies.

Yet
so often
we feel
or we are made to feel
that there is something wrong
with us.
With our tears.
So we stop.
Crying.
And in doing so
we stop
releasing.
We stop healing.
And all of the feelings
and all of the emotions

the expressions of grief
are stuffed
and stored
deep
deep
inside of us.
Sadness.
Anger.
Anguish.
Despair.
Guilt.
Rage.
Regret.
Loneliness.
Confusion.
Terror.
To name just a few.

And
in time
the weight
of these stuffed
and stored
feelings and emotions
becomes unbearable.
Exhausting.
Overwhelming.
Indescribable.
Paralyzing.
Give yourself permission to cry.

Cry.
Cry.

Cry.

Someone you love dearly
has died.

Remind yourself
over
and over
and over again
that crying is tangible sign
that you are healing.

Crying is your body's way
of releasing all the crap
that has been stuffed
and stored
deep inside you.

Crying is your body's way
of making room.
Of clearing the space
and making room
for new life
and for new love.□
For a new you.

Cry.
Cry.
Cry.

And as the tears fall
let the voice inside your head
say

I am healing.
I am healing.
I am healing.

Let the voice inside your head say
This is sacred.
This is transformational.

I am healing.
I am healing.
I am healing.

When someone you love
dearly
dies
it is okay to cry.
It is helpful to cry.
It is healing to cry.

Give yourself permission to cry.
As often as you want to.
As often as you need to.
Honor these sacred moments.

16. HAVE MERCY

I invite you to rest
your mind
from the torturous thoughts
and the painful beliefs
that may be
swirling inside your head.

Why did I ignore the signs?

Why didn't I insist that he see the doctor sooner?

Why didn't I take her seriously?

I should have been able to save him.

A good mother does not let her child die.

Children from good families do not die by suicide.

I should be farther along by now.

I should have said goodbye.

I will never be able to forgive myself.

My life is horrible.
I wish I was dead.

It should have been me that died.

God is punishing me.

Etc.
Etc.
Etc.

I invite you to rest
your mind.

Then open to the possibility
that you are in the perfect place
on this grief journey of yours.

What if everything
is exactly as it should be
in order for you to heal
your broken heart?

What if every
single
step you've taken
has been perfect
and necessary?

What then?

What if it's all brought you to this moment?
This moment
where you get to choose
how
and if

you love
yourself.

What if every step has brought you to this moment
when you get to choose
peace or pain.
What if you get to choose mercy.

Mercy.

Yes
you get to choose to have mercy
on you.
You get to choose
how you want to be
and who you want to be
to you.
To yourself.
You can be
kind
compassionate
gentle
forgiving
understanding
and merciful.

Can you have mercy on yourself?□
Will you?

Can you say to yourself
over
and over
and over again

Someone I love
dearly
has died
and I did the best I could.
I did the very best I could
knowing what I knew at the time.
And now
now I'm doing the best that I can
too.
And I will continue
day-by-day
to do the best I can.
I will give myself a break
and have mercy on me. □
□
I will choose peace over pain.

I will have mercy on me.
I am doing the best I can
and it's all unfolding perfectly.

17. WHAT IS GOD?

I don't believe we were born to suffer.
I don't believe that's why we came to the planet.
That's not why we were created.
We did not come here to suffer
all the remaining days of our life.
Did we?

But we each have free will.
We are free to choose suffering
over
and over
and over again.

But why?

Why create
and repeat stories that add pain
on top of pain
on top of the pain we are already experiencing?

Why?

Why insist that *I will never forgive myself?*

Why insist that *I should have been there?*

Why insist that *I should have known?*
Why insist that *I should have said goodbye?*

Why insist on clinging to all the other beliefs
that cause us indescribable pain?

Why?

Author Richard Rohr says
We become the God we worship.

I become the God I worship.

I loved the presentation of God
in the movie
The Shack.
Papa
and Jesus
and the Holy Spirit.
To me
it is breathtaking.

Divine love.
Forgiveness.
No judgment.
Patience.
Kindness.
Joy.
Merciful.
Understanding.

I could go on
and on
but if you've seen the movie or read the book you get it.
If you haven't
you can get a sense of what I'm talking about

by the list of qualities I've used to describe
God.

With this in mind
ask yourself
What is God?

When someone we love dies
we are broken open.
We are supposed to be.
We are invited to ask and answer
what I believe are life's fundamental questions
and
perhaps the most important of all is
What is God?

Ask yourself
What is God?
And then open to the possibility
that you have created yourself
consciously
or subconsciously
in the image of the God that you believe in.

If you truly believe God is love
you will become love.
If you truly believe God is forgiving
you will forgive yourself
and all the others.

If you truly believe God does not judge
you will not judge
yourself

or any of the others.

If you truly believe God is patient
you will become patience.

If you truly believe God is kind
you will emulate kindness.

If you truly believe God is joy
you will overflow with joy.

If you truly believe God is mercy
you will have mercy on yourself
and on everyone else.

If you truly believe God is understanding
you will seek to understand.

If you truly believe God is
loving
and forgiving
and not judgmental
and patient
and kind
and joyful
and merciful
and understanding
you will offer all of that to yourself.
And to everyone you meet.
Everyone.
Not just the ones who are like you.
Everyone.

Ask your God
if you came to this planet to suffer
all the remaining days of your life.
And then listen for an answer.
Ask.
Listen.
Ask.
Listen.

Trust.

You did not come here to suffer.
You came to be radiant.
Radiant.

18. CHOOSING FREEDOM

1. No matter what I did
or didn't do
I am not responsible for your death.
I'm just not.
I release that belief.

2. If I could have saved you
I would have.
I couldn't.
In spite of everything I did
I could not save you.

3. At the time
I did the very best I could.
I will not punish myself
over
and over
and over again
for what I did and didn't do.
I release myself from that pain.

4. I loved you as best I could.
It was not perfect.
I am a human being.
I still love you.

5. You loved me as best you could.
You were not perfect.
You were a human being.

You still love me.

6. Hanging on to the pain
clinging to it in fact
does not keep me connected to you.
It keeps me in pain.
I release all that pain.

7. I forgive you for all the crap.
You did the best you could.
And I forgive me for all the crap.
I did the best I could.

8. I forgive them
too
for all the crap.
Hard as it is to say
at times
they did the best they could too.

9. I choose to be happy.
As often as I can.

10. And I'm going to continue to love you.
And remember that you love me
always.

Freedom.
It's up to me.
I choose Freedom.

I did not come to suffer.
That's not why I was born.

I came to be radiant.

19. FORGIVENESS

In order to heal
I must forgive everyone
for everything
always.

I must forgive God
the world
the system
the medical community
the drunk driver
the one with the gun
my father
my mother
my spouse
my partner
my siblings
my family
my friends
my colleagues
and my community
for whatever they did
and for whatever they didn't do.

For what they said
and for what they were unable to say.

I must forgive the one I love who died.
I must forgive my beloved.

I must forgive myself.

And most of all
I must forgive life
for being life.

20. GRATITUDE

If the only prayer you ever say in your whole life is "thank you,"
that would suffice. ~ Meister Eckhart

I love this quote.
I think it's true.
Simple.
Profound.
Complex.
Especially for those of us
learning to live with the death of someone we love
dearly.

Yes.
It's complex.

How can we be grateful
for anything
anything at all
when it feels like we've *lost*
everything?
Everything.
Our love.
Our life.
Our present.
Our future.
Everything.
How can we be thankful?
And why would we want to be thankful
anyway

when it feels like we've *lost* it all?

I'll tell you why.

We never see the world as it is.
Not really.
We see the world as we are.
Yes.
We see the world as we are.
That's why two people can see the same thing
or share the same experience
and when it's time to describe what they saw or experienced
they are miles apart.
Miles.

It's because their description
of what they saw
or the experience they shared
has much more to do
with who they are
on the inside
than what they actually saw
or experienced□
on the outside.
And when someone we love
dearly
dies
we experience lack.
We rest in a place of lack.
For a time.
Some longer than others.
And it's painful.
Lacking hurts.

I've been robbed.
She was taken from me.
I will never be happy again.
Life sucks. □
Death sucks.
Life is so cruel and unfair.
I will never heal. Ever.
There will always be a gaping hole.
Etc.
Etc.
Etc.

When we send down deep roots
in a place of lack
that becomes the lens
through which we see our own life
over
and over
and over.

We will continue to see
and experience
lack
loss
and disappointment
and not enough
and unfair
and cruel
and
and
and we become the victim.
Over
and over

and over.

When we move to a place of gratitude
the shift occurs.
I know it's not easy.
Especially at first.
But be open to the possibility
that there really is something about life
your life
to be thankful for.
And then allow yourself to go there.

You are not betraying anyone.
Feeling better
does not mean you love less.

It might start off small.
A child's hand to hold.
A bird at the window.
Laughing at a commercial on television.
A hug
a real hug
from a friend.
A ripe
juicy
tomato that you can actually taste.
A peach.
A song that brings you back.
An unexpected phone call
or email.
Someone mentions his name
or shares a story about her
that you had forgotten.

That fact that your car works
or that you have money for gas.
A roof over your head.

And on
and on.

When you allow gratitude in
the lens through which you see the world changes.
Lack begins to melt away.
And your world changes.
And then you change.
And then your world changes more.
And you change more.

It's simple.
It's profound.
It's complex.

It's okay to say yes to gratitude.
To life.
To love.
To you.
It's okay to say yes to gratitude.
Again,
or for the first time.
It's okay to offer a prayer of thanks.

21. *I AM NOT THAT POWERFUL*

One of the most painful lies
many of us
tell ourselves
over
and over
and over again
is that somehow
someway
we should have been able to save the life
of the person we love
so dearly
who died.

We tell ourselves
that it's our fault that he died.
Somehow
someway
we are responsible for her death.

We've managed to convince ourselves
that we should have known better.
We should have done better.
We should have asked better questions.
We should have said this.
Or done that.
If only.
Why didn't I?
And on
and on

and on.

The truth is
you could not save her.
And neither could I.
No matter what you did
no matter who you talked to
no matter what questions you asked
no matter how many doctors
hospitals
treatment centers
psychiatrists
residential facilities
you contacted
he still died.

The cancer spread.
He found the drugs.
The gun went off.
The diagnosis was wrong.
The treatment failed.
The options ran out.
The car spun out of control.
The plane crashed.

The truth is
neither you nor I
or anyone reading these words
was powerful enough to keep our beloved from dying.

The truth is.
The real truth is
that we would have done anything

anything
anything at all
to save his life.
To keep her here
with us.

We would have done anything.

The truth is
we are simply not that powerful.
Not one of us
not one
was able to save the life
of the one we love so dearly.
We are not that powerful.

Humbly accepting the limits
of our ability
our human ability
to keep another human being alive
brings us freedom
and peace.

Freedom and peace.
Instead of relentless
never-ending
excruciating
self-inflicted pain.

If we could have
we would have.
But not one of us
was able to keep our beloved alive.

Choose freedom.
Choose peace.
For you.

If you could have kept him alive
you would have.
If you could have kept her here with you
you would have done whatever was necessary.

You did the best you could.
You are simply not that powerful.

22. ARE YOU STILL HERE?

As adults we get to choose
what we believe.
About life.
About death.
And about what happens to us after we die.

And our choices will either create peace or pain.
Peace
or
pain.
If you've already experienced enough pain
choose peace.
Create peace.
Consciously.

Do you think the essence of who we are is eternal?
When we finish our earthly work
and leave our physical body
do we continue to exist?

When someone you love
dearly
dies
this is a very important question to ask yourself.
And to answer.
Especially if you want to make peace with life.
Your life.
If you are not certain.
I invite you to get really quiet.

To get still.
And then ask the question.
To the one you love
who left his/her physical body.

Are you still here?
Are you by my side?
Can you hear me?
And then listen
Listen.
Listen.

With new ears
and with a new heart.

This is the important part.
Your heart
your intuition
your gut
even your body
will become aware of the response.
To your question.

Are you still here?
Are you by my side?
Can you hear me?

Yes.

And in the very next second
your head
your mind
your brain

will say
That is your imagination.
That is wishful thinking.
You didn't actually hear anything.

When that happens.
Not if.
But when that happens
I want you to get really still again
and ask again.

Are you still here?
Are you by my side?
Can you hear me?

Is that really you?

Yes.
Open to the response.
Of your beloved.

Open your heart.

This takes practice at first.
Because the head
the mind
the brain will fight it.
But the heart knows.
And recognizes truth.
The heart recognizes truth
by the way it feels.
Healing occurs in the heart.
Not the head.

And in the end it is up to you
to decide what you believe.

Are we eternal beings?
Is your beloved right by your side?
Above you.
Below you.
To your left.
And to your right.
In front of you.
And behind you.

As an adult
you get to decide what you believe.

What do you choose to believe?
And does your belief create peace or pain?
For you.
Do we continue to exist?
When we finish all the work
we came here to do
and leave our physical body?
What happens next?

Is that the end?
Of us?
Is it over?
Do we cease to exist?

Or does something else happen?
Does our essence
our spirit
our energy

our life force
our soul
continue?

When someone we love
dearly
dies
the questions arise.
They are supposed to.

And in order to heal
one of the questions that needs to be answered is
Does the person you love who died
still exist
in some shape or form?

I'm not talking about
in our memories and in our heart
I'm asking
literally
do we continue to exist?

Are we eternal beings?

If you're not sure
and I understand completely if you are not
set some time aside to sit quietly today.
Get really quiet.
Still.
Focus on your breath for a while.
In and out.
In and out.
Realize that most of the time

we are each actually being breathed
by a force outside of our awareness.
We are being breathed by love itself.

When you feel still
ask your beloved
these questions.

Are you here?
Do you still exist?
Can you hear me?

Are you here?
Do you still exist?
Can you hear me?

And then listen.
Listen.
Listen.

With new ears.
With a new heart.

Listen for your beloved's response.

23. *SURROUNDED BY LIGHT*

Imagine yourself
standing in the center
of a bright
beam of light.
A beam of light
pouring forth
from a space high above you.
Your arms are outstretched
eyes closed
and your face is looking up.

You are surrounded from head to toe
by this light.
Pouring over you.
Gently circling and swirling around you.

You are completely open
and able to receive this pure white light
which is actually Divine Love.

Standing now in a pool of this light.
You feel great love.
You feel love circling
and swirling
around you.
And you realize that the source of this love
this divine love
in the form of light
is your beloved.

The one you love
so dearly
who has died.

As you completely
open to your beloved's love
for you
you realize
once and for all
that your beloved wants
or needs nothing from you.
Because that is how Divine Love is.
Divine Love wants
and needs nothing.
Ever.
It's different from human love.

Your beloved does not need you to be happy.
Your beloved does not need you to say
or do or be anything.
Your beloved does not need to forgive
or to be forgiven.
Your beloved does not want you to feel guilty
or responsible
or less than.
Your beloved surrounds you with love.
Always.
And forever.
Your beloved surrounds you with love.
Always.
And forever.

Can you feel it?

Will you feel it?

Imagine yourself standing in the center
of this beam of light.
Your arms are outstretched
your eyes closed
and your face looking up.
Breathe it in.
Breathe it in.

And come back to this space as often as you like.

24. PRESENT TENSE

How would it feel
if today
just for today
you made the conscious decision
to talk about your loved ones
the ones who died
in the present tense?

I know this is counter to what you've been taught.

But
clearly
there is a new way to do grief
which will create a new way for you
yes you
to do life
if and when you allow it.

A new way to do life.
Your life.

Our loved ones
are present
here
right now.

It is so
so
so much more than

in our hearts and memories.

That belief minimizes them
and the role they want to play in our lives.

That belief minimizes us
too.
And what we came here to do.

That belief minimizes the reason we were born.

You would not be reading these words
unless a part of you
even the smallest part
knew that.

The death of someone we love
cracks us open
inviting us to become
the person we were born to be.

How would it feel
if today
just for today
you made the conscious decision
to talk about your loved ones
the ones who died
in the present tense?

25. *LOST*

I lost my child 3 years ago.
It's been 7 weeks since we lost mom.
Child loss is the worst loss of all. □
I'll never get over the loss of my husband.
And on
and on
and on.

If you believe your beloved is lost.
Your #1 job
is to find him.
Find her.

Now.

26. WHO AM I NOW?

Who am I now?
Who am I?
I just don't know who I am anymore.

When someone we love
dearly
dies
we are cracked open.
We are shattered
in millions
and millions of pieces.
And for a time
it feels as if
we have no idea who we are now.
As the tsunami
that is grief
gains strength and power.
As the volcano
that is grief
continues to erupt
over
and over
and over again.
As the Category 5 hurricane
settles into our being
and seems to destroy everything in its path.
It is normal to think
I just don't know who I am.
Not anymore.

Who am I now?

And I'll ask the question
Who would you like to be?
Now.
Who would you like to be?
If I gathered together
the five people who know you best
living or dead
and asked them to come up with five adjectives
that describe you best
what would those adjectives be?

Kind?
Loyal?
Loving?
Patient?
Understanding?
Fun-loving?
Adventurous?
Sensitive?
A great listener?
Full of life?
Compassionate?
Gentle?
Fill in the blank _____.

How would the people who know you best
describe you?

You are still all of those things.
You still possess all of those characteristics.

So start there.
When trying to determine who you want to be now.

Ask five people
to write five adjectives
that describe you
on a 5 x 7 index card.
For five days
spend five minutes
pondering five of the adjectives.
And ask yourself
Is this true?
Is this really who I am?
You are the designer.
The architect.
The artist.
The creator of your next chapter.

And you will
design and create
this new version of you
either consciously
or subconsciously.

The death of your beloved
is transforming you
right now.
In every second
of every minute
of every hour
of every day
of every month
and

yes
in every year
you are being transformed.

Choose to design and create today
right now
with intention.

Who do you want to become?

Who are you becoming?

Who did you come to the planet to be?

27. BECOMING RADIANT

Thank you Lexi and Zach for reflecting me in your own radiant light.
Thank you for saying yes to me. Again

.

The death of someone we love
cracks us open.
It's supposed to.
It's our invitation
to become the person
we were born to be.

Four times.
Four times.
Four times.
Four times falling into the deepest
darkest
seemingly hopeless
bottomless
pit of despair.

My little brother Danny.
My daughter Erin.
My wife Trici.
My son Rory.

Four times.

The pain unspeakable.
I numbed
and repressed
and stuffed every feeling
and every emotion

in order to survive.

I didn't know any better.
How could I?
It's what we do.

That's how I did grief.
The first time.
And the second
And part of the third.
Before I knew there was
a new way.

Of course I contemplated suicide.
More than once.
I wanted to die.
The pain was that painful.
The darkness that dark.

In that darkest
that stillness
I heard a voice.
So quiet
so soft and tentative.
So fragile.
A whisper really.

Or you could choose to live.

I don't know how long I lay there
mulling over my
two options.

Life or death.
Peace or pain.
Love or fear.

I listened.

And the whisper grew
louder
and stronger
and bolder
And it became clear
that life
itself
had other plans for me.

I chose to live.
I choose to live.

A tiny
flickering
white light
at my tunnel's end
set itself ablaze
and
with my yes
my yes
the tunnel itself was lit.
The tunnel was lit.

Healing became my journey
my intention
my vision
my daily action.

Life's personal invitation
to me.

The invitation to dig deeper
to say yes
to become hope
and possibility.
To love more wildly
to choose peace instead of pain
as often as possible.
To forgive.
To become light.
To return to love.
To become
radiant.

Again.

We were not born to suffer.
That is not why we came.
We are
each
stronger than we think.
Stronger than we know.
Stronger than we believe.

We have walked through fire
and we can do it again
and again
and again.

Life itself is whispering:

I am not done with you.
I am not done with you.

You have more to experience,
more to explore
more to discover
more to create
more to enjoy
more to love

You were born to be radiant.
And so was I.
Not in spite of the fact that someone we love has died,
but because of the fact that someone we love has died.

We have walked through fire
we have braved the open flames
we have welcomed with open arms
and open hearts
the darkness
the pain
the sorrow
the light
the love
the joy.

All gifts
yes gifts
that death
and grief
and life itself offer.

We are not weak.

Far from it.

We have said yes.
When so many say no.

We have said yes.
To life.
To love.
To our very selves.

To being cracked open
and to radiantly becoming
the people we were born to be.

We were born to be radiant.

Radiant.

That's why we came.

That's who we are.

28. WE ARE LOVED THAT MUCH

Every person we encounter.
Every single one.
Every experience.
Every triumph.
Every crushing blow.
Every mountain we climb.
From the moment we are conceived.
Every mountain we fall from.
Till we leave our physical body.

Every birth.
Every "death."

It all happens for us.
Not to us.
We are loved that much.

Every emotional high.
Every psychological expansion.
Every spiritual awakening.
Every physical personal best.
For us.
Not to us.

Every depressing episode.
Every psychological wound.
Every spiritual desert.
Every physical break.
For us.

Not to us.
We are loved that much.

Grief is not the enemy.
Pain is not the enemy.
Nothing.
Nothing.
Nothing is to be avoided.

Grief
and pain
are the doors we enter
to find truth.
To create the miracle.
To shift our perception.
Our path to peace.
And love.

Life is not good or bad.
Life is not right or wrong.
Life is not appropriate or inappropriate.
These are all man-made judgments.

The Universe does not judge.
The Universe Is Creation Itself.

We are creation.
The creators.
With every breath.
With every breath we take.
Consciously
or subconsciously.

And we get to choose.
To be awake.
Or remain asleep.

Most of us create subconsciously.
We remain asleep.
Most of us create pain
on top of pain
on top of pain.

Rooted in fear.

Until we don't anymore.

Until the pain is so great
so unbearable
so unimaginable
so indescribable
that we raise our head
look up
and say
There must be a new way.

There is.
And it is rooted in deep love
and compassion
and understanding
and wisdom
and gentleness
and asking all the questions
and listening for the answers.

There is a new way to do life.

It is rooted in knowing
and remembering
and choosing to believe
over
and over
and over again
that we did not come here to suffer.
Choosing
deciding
to believe that truth
until we reawaken
reignite
reclaim
the flame
which has been burning
deep inside our being
since the beginning of time.

We did not come here to suffer.
Not one of us.
We came to be radiant.
To live our optimal life.
We are loved that much.

We are loved that much.

The greatest gift you can give yourself.
Your family.
Your friends.
Your colleagues.
Your community
your church
and your town.

The greatest gift you can give the world
the entire world
the seen
and the unseen
is to heal your broken heart
your broken spirit
your broken dream.

As you heal
I heal.
And as I heal
you heal.

We are all connected.

We came to the planet to be radiant.
Radiant.
Be Radiant.
Live your optimal life.

We came to the planet to be radiant.

There is a new way.
There is a new way to do life.

ACKNOWLEDGEMENTS

The world told me I was a man with a dead wife and two dead kids. I believed that. For many years. Without question. Why wouldn't I? And that belief created pain on top of pain on top of pain. I didn't know any better.

One day, I decided that I had suffered enough. I began to search for a new way. First I searched for a new way to do grief. And when I discovered that, I continued to search. For a new way to do life. When I discovered that. Finally. I wrote this book. For you. Like me, you have suffered enough.

And I have so, so, so many people to give thanks to.

To Trici for saying yes. Over and over and over again. Always to life. When some of the kids at school ruthlessly and viscously tormented you because your skin was porcelain white. *You don't look like us,* they taunted. You not only said yes, but you made the conscious decision, from that moment on, to welcome everyone. Everyone. Always. And you did.

When you decided to pattern your life after Bobby Kennedy's life and you became a *voice for the voiceless.* Your voice, your work, your life became your yes. □
□
When you discovered that the first man you thought you would marry cheated on you and broke your heart. You said yes. *I will love again.* And you did.

When you said yes to me. To our first lunch. Our first date. And six weeks later to my proposal. When you took me to

Ireland on our honeymoon, insisting we stay in castles. Ashford. Belleek. Ballynahinch. Yes. Yes. Yes.

When you slowly said yes to life after Erin left her physical body. At 5:10 pm on July 18, 1990. That hot, sticky Chicago summer afternoon. And when you said yes to another baby. Rory Brennan Zuba. And another. Sean Brennan Zuba.

If you had not said yes. Over and over and over again, this book would not have been born. Thank you Trici. A million, million times thank you.

To Erin. For coming. Again. Thank you.

To Rory. My most amazing son. For teaching me how thrilling it can be to be fully alive. Thank you.

And to Sean. **My greatest teacher.** The one who said, *I will walk side-by-side with him. I will make sure he stays on the planet.* I did. I have. I am so very grateful. Thank you. I love you now and forever. Forever.

To every person who said yes to me. And to every person who said hell to the no to me.

To my family. My grandparents. Especially my grandma, my mom's mom, Ciss Mcinnerney - for delighting in who I am. Thank you.

To Trici's family. To the kid's daycare providers, Marilyn and Tami. To Trici's many friends. Especially Nancy. And Rita, who left the planet the same way Rory did - a glioblastoma. To Lynne and Chip. And Lili and Patty. And Renee and Patti. To

Jaunita, arm-in-arm with Trici now. You saw Erin before she was born. Thank you.

To my tightest circle of friends. It could not have been easy, to keep moving in close, when so, so, so many ran far away. To Paula, and Ann and Cathy. To Joan and Amy, and Luanne. Thank you.

To Sue and Bob for introducing me to Terrie the Tucson healer. You changed the trajectory of my life so soon after Trici died. Thank you.

To Gary and Linda and everyone who said yes to those first Intensives at Mt. Madonna. And to my soul circle partners in Walnut Creek, CA. Thank you.

To Naheed for teaching me that I could love again. And for showing me what love in action is. Again. To your mom and dad for loving The Professor and Sunshine. Thank you.

To my Walnut Creek family. You saved our lives. Jeannie and Marina and Ann and Kay and Joanne and Kathryn. To Scotty, and Tomas and Andrew and Marianna, and Tommy and Johnny and Samuel, and Trent and Eric, and Ben and Felicia, and Zach. Thank you.

To Chris Zydel for waking up and shaking up the artist in me. To Jean for introducing me to Chris. To Tamara for walking by my side. Thank you.

To Cindy. We spent 9-11 together. For us, a normal day. Thank you.

To Natalie Rogers for introducing me to your beloved father Carl's work. And to Expressive Arts. And to the incredible cohort at Westerbeke Ranch. You all continue to help me heal. Thank you.

To my high school friends who held me when I came back home. Broken. I feel 16 when I am with you. Thank you.

To Beth for being you. Thank you.

To Maureen. Since Sophomore year. Thank you.

To my college friends. My Newman Center family. I loved that time in our lives. Thank you.

And to everyone in Rockford who stepped in closer as Rory got sicker. And stepped in even closer after he died. To Sheri and Greg and Matthew and Carrie and Joey. To Mary Jo. And Anna and Mary and Linda. To Richard and Libby. And Peggy and John. To Jude for walking with me. To Jackie. Thank you.

To Ila for putting me back together. Thank you.

To Jasmine and Jen and Therese and Meg. The power of touch and intention to heal. And to Kathy. Thank you.

To Elaine and Dorothy for creating such a safe, sacred space. Thank you.

To Ellen and Dave and Nick and Andrew and Luke. For creating a family for Sean when I could not. Thank you.

To Jared and all the incredible people at The Fit. When my mind and spirit were broken you helped my build up my body. Thank you.

To Shawn, and Tom and Tracy. Rockford's version of The Rat Pack. And to Cindy and Mrs. M. for allowing us to be boys again.

To Shelby. For designing my book cover. For loving Molly and Sean. Thank you.

To Jeri and Jim, and Teagan and Zach and Leo and Karen for bringing us together. Thank you.

To my Shamans - Annette, and Rick and your loving wife Beth. To Carol and Rita for introducing me to Annette. To Susan for introducing me to Rick. To Jessica and Joshua for making it crystal clear that I was to work with your mommy and daddy. Thank you.

To Ethan for bringing Erik and Jessica to me. Thank you.

To Sophie for bringing me Gretchen and Scott and Holly and Bob. Thank you.

To all my clients. To your spouses. Your children. Your parents. To all your beloveds who left the planet at the perfect time in the perfect way and brought us together. Thank you.

To Oprah Winfrey for introducing me to such powerful teachers. My work is rooted in their work. I stand on their shoulders. To Gary Zukav and Debbie Ford and Marianne Williamson and Byron Katie and Maya Angelou and Don

Miguel Ruiz and Collin Tipping and Eckhart Tolle and Iyanla Vanzant. Thank you.

To John E. Welshons, and Emmanuel, and Leonard Jacobson, and Stephen Levine, and Wayne Dyer. and Michael Beckwith and Rickie Byars Beckwith. Your work has touched my heart and informed my work. Thank you.

To Amy and Paula for painstakingly and lovingly editing this manuscript. And Anna for sweeping in at the last minute!!! Thank you.

To Charlie. For bringing Lexi and Zach to help me. Your vision is breathtaking. To Lincoln, you sweet soul. Thank you.

To the fourteen brave souls who said yes to my first Becoming Radiant retreat. You know who you are, and so do I. You are the pioneers. Thank you.

To Kim and Kirk for standing by my side. To Garrett. Thank you.

To every soul who will read these words. Thank you for co-creating this book with me.

To life itself. For being life. For me. Not to me. Thank you.

ABOUT THE PAINTING

The painting on the cover of this book is mine. I am the artist.

Thank you Francis Rothluebber for becoming who you are. For helping my mom and dad after Erin died. For facilitating that retreat I attended at Jim and Sally, and Frank and Renee, and Fred and Karen, and Carol and Don's sacred space.

Thank you Sue for remembering I was there. At the retreat. And to Jan; Rory's classmate Kristen's mom, for sending my blog to Jessica. The one about being cracked open. She was. After her son Ethan died. Thank you Sue for stopping by our house. And leaving your business card with Sean. *Please call.* I did.

My grandson Ethan died. My daughter-in-law Jessica read your words. She wants to meet you. Will you help her and my son Erik? I will. I did. For 18 months. Every Tuesday. Two hours a night.

Thank you Jessica and Erik. For saying yes. Over and over and over again. When so many would have said no. Just no. No. This is way too hard. And thank you Blake, Chase and Bodey. For lending me your mommy and daddy.

Thank you Jessica for allowing me to help you create our Restoring A Mother's Heart retreats. Sponsored by The Ethan A. Lindberg Foundation. For moms of kids who died from a chronic illness. We offered four retreats. At The Abbey in Lake Geneva, WI. Of all the things I'd been involved with, these retreats rose quickly to the top of my list. We tinkered with the second retreat. *How can we make it more meaningful? More healing?* We added a painting activity. And some wine. During the afternoon of the second day.

Paint this answer. ***Where is your beloved?*** *Now. Now that they've left their physical body. Where are they now?* It's an essential question To ask. And answer. If you want to create peace. There isn't a right answer, or a wrong answer. All that matters is that you find your answer. ***Where is your beloved?***

I've known where my beloveds, my people - Erin and Trici and Rory - are for a long time. They're in the presence of the Divine. Where all things are possible. All things. Unlimited possibility.

So I painted that. On a 2' x 3' canvas. In yellow. And white. And shades of orange. In colors that are … radiant. It sits in my living room.

And that painting is the cover of this book. I am the artist.

ABOUT THE AUTHOR

Tom Zuba is one of the lucky ones. He knows exactly why he was born. Tom came to Planet Earth to transform the way we do grief worldwide; to teach those learning to live with the death of someone they love A New Way to Do Grief which creates A New Way to Do Life. Tom's teachings are based on the knowledge, wisdom and tools he continues to gain as he learns to live with the "death" of his 18-month-old daughter Erin in 1990, his 43-year-old wife Trici in 1999, and his 13-year-old son Rory in 2005.

Tom is convinced that none of us came here to suffer. That is not why we came. We were born to be radiant. Not in spite of the fact that someone we love died. But because of the fact that someone we love died.

Tom is the author of the #1 best-selling book *Permission to Mourn: A New Way to Do Grief.* He is a life coach and speaker who travels all over the world teaching people how to heal themselves. He works with clients one-on-one. He creates and facilitates online programs. personal retreats, day-long seminars and workshops for medical professionals and the general public. Tom and his son Sean are consciously creating radiant lives in Rockford, Illinois. To learn more visit TomZuba.com and find Tom at www.facebook.com/tomzuba1

☐

☐

Praise for □
Permission to Mourn ~ □
A New Way to Do Grief□

available at Amazon and bookstores everywhere.□
□

"I recommend with joy Tom Zuba's exquisite, perceptive, and profound celebration of life, *Permission to Mourn*. Despite its title, it is actually a book about permission to live. It takes us where we all need to go and gently, kindly shows us a path." ~ Gary Zukav, author of *The Seat of the Soul* and *Spiritual Partnership*.

"This is undoubtedly one of the finest books I've ever read about grief, and trust me, I've read dozens of them. Tom Zuba speaks with the authentic voice of one who knows first-hand the experience of unspeakable loss, not only as a twice-bereaved parent but as a surviving spouse as well. The content is clinically accurate and reliable, in that it reflects the most current research and thinking of noted experts in the field of grief and loss. What is more, it is delivered in a manner that is filled with hope, wisdom and love. I will not hesitate to recommend it highly to clients and colleagues. If you know someone who is grieving, I cannot think of a more thoughtful gift than this beautiful book." ~ Marty Tousley, Grief Counselor

"This book completely changed my life." ~ Kathie

"My son died of a heroin overdose in May of 2016. This book was originally given to me by my sister the day of Neil's memorial. It took almost a month to gather the courage to even open the book but once I started I couldn't put it down until I finished it. It is easy to read and well written so that you can read and digest the information a little at a time. It had such a healing effect on me that I have made a ministry of giving copies away to anyone I meet that is fighting to survive the death of a loved one. I highly recommend it to everyone." ~ Debbie

"I gift this book to friends when a loved one has died. This is so well written and a soothing balm to the grieving soul." ~ Pookie

"What can I say to help you believe that this book WILL bring you peace, clarity, insight, and hope during your time of grief? Perhaps nothing more than it gave me just that. How is this book different? It is written clearly, yet poetically in chunks that are not too large for one to digest. You find yourself rereading a passage and getting a deeper understanding each time. It has been my bedside companion since losing my husband to suicide in May. Death can make you feel lost. Death can make you feel hopeless. However, death is as natural as birth and life, so it doesn't have to feel that way forever. This book will give you permission to look at death differently. It is this man's life experience with death that has allowed him to become such a comfort to others." ~ Shari

"Outstanding book...it speaks to your heart and puts into words what you are feeling...just excellent! I shared this with my grief group and all 13 love it!" ~ Cathleen

"You saved my life!" ~ Mary

"PRECIOUS WISDOM gleaned by going through the fires of hell after losing his daughter, his wife and his son over the course of years. I just discovered this book, nine years after losing my 21-year old son to a congenital heart condition. Wish it existed back in 2008. It resonates, and many of his suggested ways of dealing with "the death of someone you love, dearly" I was aware of (I'm a therapist). FEEL ALL YOUR FEELINGS. I knew this, but many people don't know that this is the ONLY way to keep going forward and come through with sanity, courage and grace. I also love his suggestion (not a lecture, just a suggestion) to imagine that your loved one is close by, always with you. The very night I finished reading this book, I had a dream about my son, (which doesn't happen very often now, though I had many dreams of him in the early years), with me asking "Where are you?" and he answered, "Right here!" I'm buying copies of this book to share with other grieving mothers I know." ~ P. Parkin

"BEST book in the world. For almost 8 years I have been living with survivor guilt...this book has allowed me to move forward in life." ~ Melissa

"Having just lost my son, I found *Permission to Mourn* very helpful and comforting as I faced this very painful period. I wish Tom Zuba was able to learn these personal lessons without having to lose his baby daughter, his wife and young son, but his painful lessons were appreciated by me as I faced my personal loss. Thank you, Tom!!" ~ Thomas

"Love his book!! It definitely brought me out of my darkness." ~ Melinda

"I have purchased over a dozen books. When I first read this, I knew I had confirmation I wasn't alone or crazy in my thoughts and feelings. I have given this to my children and close friends that have suffered deep losses. Everyone has been grateful." ~ Joanne.